CELTIC SAINTS

ILLUSTRATED BY *Ann MacDuff*

CHRONICLE BOOKS

SAN FRANCISCO

First published in 1995 by
The Appletree Press Ltd., 19–21 Alfred Street,
Belfast BT2 8DL
Tel. +44 (0) 1232 243074
Fax +44 (0) 1232 246756
Copyright © The Appletree Press Ltd. 1995
Printed in the E.U. All rights reserved.
No part of this publication may be
reproduced or transmitted in any form
or by any means, electronic or mechanical,
photocopying, recording or any information
and retrieval system, without permission
in writing from the publisher.

Celtic Saints

First published in the United States in 1995
by Chronicle Books, 275 Fifth Street,
San Francisco, CA 94103

ISBN: 0-8118-1178-6

9 8 7 6 5 4 3 2 1

THE CELTIC CHURCH

O f all the saints in this book, Patrick must be the best known. His feast day, 17 March, is celebrated wherever the Irish and their descendants gather. To Patrick is attributed the conversion of Ireland's pagan Celtic tribes to Christianity, and Ireland was to become the heartland of the Celtic Church. The legions of the Roman Empire never reached Ireland, and in consequence the Church developed an organisation largely free from papal influence and characterised by the proliferation of monasteries. This was true of other Celtic regions on the periphery of Western Europe, notably Scotland and Wales, where Roman rule was incomplete.

With the collapse of the Roman Empire, it was the Celtic Church which kept the flame of Christianity burning. In the sixth and seventh centuries its missionaries travelled throughout Europe in their battle against paganism. Most of the saints in this book belong to that golden age of the Celtic Church. Their stories can only be a mixture of fact and legend. Fact is certainly discernible in the stone remains of their buildings, less often in the fanciful biographies written centuries after their deaths. But where there are tales of miracles, who is to know where truth ends and myth begins?

CIARÁN OF SAIGHER

Christianity reached Ireland some years before Saint Patrick, and Ciarán has been called the first-born of the Irish saints. Of royal blood, he was born on Clear Island, the most southerly tip of Ireland. He had an early affinity with animals, and one legend recounts that he prayed for a small bird which had been seized from its nest by a hawk. The hawk laid its bleeding prey at Ciarán's feet, and it immediately recovered.

After studying at Tours and Rome, where he was ordained a bishop, Ciarán chose a hermit's life in the Irish Midlands. His only companions in the Slieve Bloom mountains were animals, and it is said that a wild boar tore down branches to build the saint's first shelter. In time Ciarán gathered followers, and founded the monastery of Saigher, Co. Offaly, which also became the burial place of the kings of Ossory. An associated convent was led by his mother, Liadan.

In most of the miracles attributed to Ciarán he restored life to the dead; in one, seven harpers who had been murdered by robbers, joined him as monks in gratitude. But he could also cast spells, and once showed his disapproval of King Ailill by silencing his voice for a week.

DECLAN OF ARDMORE

Declan was a prince of the Decies kingdom in Munster, and his birth was accompanied by a phenomenal light in the sky. He was baptised by a Christian priest named Colman, and studied under a sage called Dioma. As a young man, he travelled to Rome and was consecrated a bishop by the Pope.

The saint possessed a miraculous black bell, with which he summoned up an empty ship to carry him back to Ireland. When one of his retinue left the bell behind on a rock, Declan prayed to God and the rock floated out to sea. Declan followed it and it eventually led him to shore at Ardmore, Co. Waterford. There, in the fifth century, Declan built his church and monastery. In later life the saint was credited with raising from the dead many who had died in a plague at Cashel, Co. Tipperary.

As well as Saint Declan's Church (known as the Cathedral) and the Oratory (housing his tomb), Ardmore now has a fine round tower. The large stone on the nearby strand is said to be the one which carried the saint's bell, and many believe that it can cure the rheumatism of those who crawl under it.

PATRICK OF IRELAND

Much of Patrick's life is shrouded in mystery and historians differ on the probable chronology of the saint's life. Fortunately, he has left behind two documents, his *Confession* and his *Letter to Coroticus,* which describe some of his experiences. He was not the first Christian missionary to reach Ireland, but the principal credit for converting the pagan island and establishing the Celtic Church belongs to him.

He was the son of a Roman official, Calpurnius, living probably in Wales. As a boy of sixteen, Patrick was captured by raiders and sold to an Irish chieftain, Milchu. He spent years in slavery, herding sheep on Slemish Mountain in Co. Antrim. He escaped following a dream in which a voice told him a ship would be waiting to take him to his own country. After a journey of 200 miles he found the ship, and was eventually able to return to his family.

One night, in a dream, he heard voices calling him back to Ireland. It is thought that he studied under Saint Germanus at Auxerre, France, and that his mission to Ireland was approved due to the early death of Saint Palladius, who had been sent as a bishop to the Irish "believing in Christ" in 431. Consequently, 432 is the traditional date for Patrick's voyage to Ireland, which ended on the shores of Strangford Lough. He quickly made a convert of a local chief named Dichu, who gave him a barn at Saul, Co. Down, for his first church.

Before long Patrick made his way to the Hill of Tara, Co. Meath, seat of the high king of Ireland. Arriving on the eve of Easter, he lit a paschal fire on the nearby Hill of Slane. At this time of year, it was pagan practice to put out all fires before a new one was lit at Tara. When the druids at Tara saw the light from Slane, they warned King Laoghaire that he must extinguish it or it would burn for ever. Patrick was summoned to Tara, and on the way he and his followers chanted the hymn known as "The Lorica" or "Saint Patrick's Breastplate". Although Laoghaire remained a pagan, he was so impressed by the saint that he gave him permission to make converts throughout his realm. Muirchu's *Life of Patrick*, written two centuries later, describes a contest of magic in which Laoghaire's druids had to concede victory to the saint.

Patrick travelled widely in Ireland, making converts and establishing new churches, though he eventually made his headquarters at Armagh. On one occasion he spent the forty days of Lent on a mountain in Co. Mayo which is now called Croagh Patrick. He was harassed by demons in the form of blackbirds, clustered so densely that the sky was black, but he continued to pray, and rang his bell to disperse the assailants. An angel then appeared to tell the saint that all his petitions for the Irish people would be granted, and that they would retain their Christian faith until Judgment Day. There are many legends about Patrick, not least that he banished snakes from Ireland and that he adopted the shamrock as a symbol of the Holy Trinity.

Patrick's writings belong to the latter part of his life and confirm that he was less learned as a writer than he was persuasive as a speaker. Nonetheless, the *Confession*, a response to criticisms of his mission in Ireland, is a moving revelation of his vocation and of the divine guidance he received in dreams. Irish annals give the date of Patrick's death as 493, but an earlier date of 461 seems more likely. Tradition says he died at Saul and was buried at nearby Downpatrick.

BRIGID OF KILDARE

Although Brigid is probably the best-known Irish saint after Patrick, her life cannot be documented with much certainty. Cogitosus's *Life of Brigid* was written not much more than a century after her death, but he was mainly concerned with recounting her many miracles. She may have been born in Co. Kildare, *c.* 457, but local tradition suggests Faughart, Co. Louth. Her parents, Dubtach and Brocseach, may both have belonged to noble families, though one account suggests that Brigid's mother was a slave in Dubtach's household. It is generally accepted that Brocseach was a Christian. Dubtach may also have been one, or perhaps converted from paganism in later life. Brigid was noted for her generosity to the poor, and as a child once gave away her mother's whole store of butter. Fortunately her prayers were answered, and the store of butter was miraculously renewed.

Her father may well have welcomed her decision to take the veil, once she had rejected his choice of a husband for her. With seven other young women robed in white, she took her vows before Saint Mel, the abbot and bishop of Longford, and it is said that he mistakenly consecrated her a bishop. When seeking land for her community, she asked the King of Leinster only for as much as her cloak would cover. The cloak miraculously spread over the whole of the Curragh, an area of grassland famous then and now for horse-racing.

In Ireland Christianity did not supplant paganism so much as superimpose itself on Celtic tradition. Sites of pagan worship or superstition quickly became associated with Christian worship and belief. Brigid's feast day, for example, falls on 1 February, the date of Imbolg, the pagan festival of spring. Significantly Brigid was also the name of a pagan goddess, and even seems to have been used as a general name for Irish goddesses, for the name means "exalted one". The attributes of the pagan Brigid, such as healing powers, learning and poetic skill, were readily perceived in the saint who established a convent at Kildare. The name Kildare means "church of the oak", and there was probably a pagan sanctuary there with a sacred fire which burned for centuries into the Christian era. By the time of Brigid's death, *c.* 525, Kildare had become an important centre of learning.

The saint travelled by chariot throughout Ireland, carrying on Patrick's work of conversion, but there is no evidence that they ever met. Many miracles of healing are attributed to Brigid, such as curing lepers and giving speech to the dumb. There are tales of her turning water into ale or stone into salt, and many concern her rapport with animals. She also negotiated the release of captives. Perhaps the best-known story is of her visit to a dying pagan chieftain. While she prayed, she plaited rushes into a cross. The chieftain heard her account of the cross as a Christian symbol, and was converted and baptised before he died. It is still customary on 1 February to plait Saint Brigid's Crosses, in the hope that they will protect a household in the year ahead.

Brigid has been called "Mary of the Gaels" and a common salutation in the Irish language expresses the hope that "Brigid and Mary be with you". Her influence is not confined to Ireland, however, for she has been revered throughout the ages in innumerable countries. One legend is that the medieval Knights of Chivalry chose Saint Brigid as their patroness, and that it was they who first chose to call their wives "brides".

ITA OF KILLEEDY

Like Saint Declan, Ita belonged to the royal family of the Decies kingdom. She was born *c.* 480 in Co. Waterford, and was baptised Deirdre. The name Ita, which she later acquired, signified her "thirst for Divine Love". When her Christian father sought to arrange her marriage to a noble youth, she fasted in protest. Her prayers were answered when an angel appeared to her father persuading him that she must be allowed to pursue her holy vocation.

Ita established a community of nuns at Killeedy, Co. Limerick. Saint Brendan was a pupil of Ita, and when, in later life, he asked her what three things were most pleasing to God, she cited true faith, simplicity and generosity. Most hateful were churlishness, love of evil and greed.

Her life was austere, and she fasted rigorously. When a rich man pressed gold on her, she immediately sent for water to wash her hands. Ita is said to be the author of an Irish lullaby, which she sang when the infant Jesus appeared to her. She died *c.* 570, perhaps from cancer; legend says that a beetle devoured her side, growing to the size of a pig.

FINNIAN OF CLONARD

Finnian is generally regarded as the father of Irish monasticism. He was born in Co. Meath towards the end of the fifth century and it is said that all the birds of Ireland gathered as a portent of the holy life he would lead. As a young man he founded three churches in Ireland before being attracted to monastic life in Wales. He studied under Saint Cadoc at Llancarfan, Glamorganshire, and was much influenced by Cadoc's pupil Gildas, who was critical of the worldliness and wealth of British bishops.

Finnian became convinced that the ascetic life offered the best way of consecrating one's life to God. It was a belief well-suited to Ireland, with its population dispersed in small rural kingdoms. Finnian's first monastery was at Aghowle, Co. Wicklow, but he settled *c.* 520 at Clonard, Co. Meath, on the River Boyne. Clonard became the most famous monastic school of the sixth century, its importance derived from the number of disciples who left to found other monasteries. Finnian's most prominent pupils have been called the twelve apostles of Ireland. The saint died of plague *c.*549, but the monastery at Clonard survived until the sixteenth century.

Brioc of Saint Brieuc

L ittle is known for certain of Brioc's life, though the saint is revered in Wales, Cornwall and Brittany. He was born in Cardiganshire during the fifth century. According to a fanciful *Life* written centuries later, an angel told his pagan parents, Cerpus and Eldruda, to send their son to be instructed by Saint Germanus in Paris. On one occasion, chastised for giving away a pitcher to lepers, he prayed and was rewarded by the miraculous appearance of a beautiful brass replacement. Through tales of his great charity, Brioc has become the patron saint of purse-makers.

He settled in Wales, but many years later was bidden by an angel to sail to France. His ship struck a sea monster, which vanished in response to Brioc's prayers. The saint first landed in Cornwall, where a local chieftain named Conan was converted when he saw how Brioc had tamed a pack of wolves threatening the aged saint in his chariot. Reaching Brittany, Brioc founded a monastery at Tréguier, but was called back to Wales to combat a plague with prayer. Returning to Brittany, he founded an abbey on the site of the present cathedral city of Saint Brieuc, where he died.

BRENDAN THE NAVIGATOR

Of all Irish saints, Brendan was the greatest traveller. He was born near Tralee, Co. Kerry, an event reputedly marked by angels hovering in a bright light over the house. He was baptised by Bishop Erc, who ensured that a year later Brendan was delivered into the care of Saint Ita at Killeedy. At the age of six Brendan returned to Erc, who undertook his education for several years before indulging the boy's desire to travel and study under other holy men. Erc asked only that he could perform his pupil's ordination as a priest, and Brendan duly returned for this ceremony. Among the Irish saints Brendan visited were Finnian of Clonard, Enda of Aran and Jarlath of Tuam.

From an early age Brendan attracted disciples, and he established a number of monasteries in Ireland. The most famous was Clonfert, Co. Galway, which was founded *c.* 560, towards the end of the saint's life. Clonfert became one of Ireland's greatest monastic schools and endured until the sixteenth century. Today, Saint Brendan's Cathedral in Clonfert is noted for its magnificent Romanesque doorway. Brendan also founded a convent at Annaghdown, Co. Galway, over which his sister Brig presided. Many landmarks of western Ireland are named after the saint, including Mount Brandon in Co. Kerry.

Brendan is associated with a number of monastic sites close to the River Shannon and around the west coast of Ireland. In addition, he voyaged to Scotland, founding a monastery on Arran and visiting other islands. He is said to have met Saint Columba on Hynba Island in Scotland, and even to have gone to Brittany with Saint Malo, a Welsh monk. He may also have stayed at Llancarfan, the Welsh monastery founded by Saint Cadoc.

Brendan's reputation as a traveller rests, however, on the *Navigatio Sancti Brendani*, an account written by an Irish monk in the ninth or tenth century. More than 100 medieval Latin manuscripts of this *Voyage of Saint Brendan* still exist, and there are versions in Middle English, French, German, Italian, Flemish and other languages. The story has been much embroidered from its original factual basis and it is impossible to separate fact and fancy. However, an epic modern voyage led by Tim Severin in the 1970s showed that it was possible to sail a coracle of wood and leather to America, and consequently that Irish monks might indeed have preceded Christopher Columbus by several centuries.

On the 3200-foot high summit of Mount Brandon are the ruins of a small beehive-shaped chapel commanding views of up to 100 miles in distance. There, it is said, the saint had a vision of the Promised Land. (There are, incidentally, many recorded accounts of the sighting of an island, a mirage usually identified as the fabled Hy-Brasil, off the west coast of Ireland.) Brendan's first attempt to sail to the Promised Land was apparently unsuccessful, but he was not discouraged. He and his crew of monks prayed and fasted for forty days, and set off on a second voyage which lasted seven years and probably took them to Iceland, Greenland and even the American mainland.

The *Navigatio Sancti Brendani* describes meetings with Saint Patrick and Judas Iscariot, the latter clinging to a rock during a temporary release from Hell. The saint celebrates Easter on the back of a whale, and escapes a predatory sea-cat as big as a horse. It is a work in the tradition of Homer's *Odyssey,* and draws on Celtic mythology as well as classical sources and the Scriptures. Many medieval cartographers included Brendan's island on their maps. In later life Brendan returned to his work in Ireland and died there in 578 at Annaghdown.

GILDAS THE WISE

Gildas was born *c.* 500 in the Clyde valley, but as a child left Scotland and studied under both Saint Illtyd and Saint Cadoc in South Wales. According to one legend, Illtyd dwelt on a narrow and squalid island, but through the prayers of Gildas and other disciples the sea withdrew and the enlarged island blossomed with flowers. Gildas is best-known for *De excidio et conquestu Britanniae* (On the Ruin and Conquest of Britain), a powerful criticism of the decadent lives of British kings and clergy, whom he blamed for the successes of Anglo-Saxon invaders.

Gildas also preached in the northern parts of Britain, and seems to have been an influential figure in the Irish Church, teaching for a time at Armagh. He later sailed to Brittany, living as a hermit on the Isle of Houat before being persuaded by local fishermen to found a monastery at Rhuys. He died in Brittany *c.* 570. To Gildas is attributed a Lorica, possibly composed when plague threatened Brittany, which itemises every part of the body in its prayer for protection. It is said that, if repeated frequently, it will add seven years to your life and that you will not die on a day when it is repeated.

CIARÁN OF CLONMACNOISE

A carpenter's son, Ciarán was born *c.* 512 in Co. Roscommon, and studied under Saint Finnian at Clonard. Like several other saints, Ciarán had an affinity with animals, it is said that a fox had been his companion in childhood and that during his time at Clonard, he would rest his book on the antlers of a tame stag. Ciarán also visited the monasteries of Saint Enda in the Aran Islands and Saint Senan on Scattery Island, Co. Clare. The first monastery he founded was on Hare Island in Lough Ree, but it was farther down the River Shannon that he began the monastery of Clonmacnoise, *c.* 545.

On the Aran Islands Ciarán had dreamed of a great fruit tree overlooking a river: Clonmacnoise was the realisation of that dream, for it became one of the great schools of Europe. In Ireland it was second only to Armagh and as a centre of literature and art it was unequalled, as evidenced by surviving manuscripts and artefacts, including the high crosses and grave-slabs which still grace the site. It was unusual, too, in that its abbots were often of humble origins like the founder. Ciarán, unfortunately, did not live to see the full flowering of Clonmacnoise, for he died seven months after work began.

DAVID OF WALES

Since the twelfth century David has been regarded as the patron saint of Wales. While all the other Celtic saints in this book enjoyed varying degrees of veneration and fame during their lives and after, David is distinguished by the fact that he was formally canonised by Pope Callistus II in 1120. Two pilgrimages to his shrine were counted the equivalent of one pilgrimage to Rome, and Kings William I, Henry II and Edward I are all said to have undertaken the journey to Pembrokeshire.

Few details of David's life can be asserted with certainty. He was probably born early in the sixth century, and was the son of a Welsh chieftain named Sant. His mother was Saint Non, a Welsh nun who appears to have worked in both Cornwall and Brittany, probably after Sant's death. David studied under Saint Illtyd, was ordained, and then spent ten years with Paulinus, a Welsh saint who had also been Illtyd's pupil and a contemporary of Saint Gildas. It is said that Paulinus became blind, and that David touched his eyes and restored his sight.

Eventually, following the guidance of an angel, David founded a monastery at Mynyw (now Saint David's) in south-west Wales. His community was noted for its austerity. The monks cultivated the land without the assistance of oxen. They spoke to one another only when necessary and were expected to pray constantly, even at work. They ate no meat products, limiting themselves to bread and vegetables. They drank only water, which is probably why their abbot became known as David the Waterman, though he was also given to immersing himself in cold water. In another legend David splashed water at his baptism, curing a bishop's blindness. David was consecrated a bishop, one legend suggesting this occurred during a pilgrimage to Jerusalem. However, it is unlikely that he left Mynyw for long, for he preferred the contemplative life. He is credited with founding ten monasteries, among them Glastonbury.

A *Life of David*, written in the eleventh century, recounts that he was so humble that he three times refused to attend the Synod of Brefi. The synod may have been called to counter a revival of the so-called "Pelagian heresy", named after the fifth-century monk Pelagius, who dismissed the idea of original sin and the consequent need for redemption. Eventually Paulinus suggested sending two saints, Deiniol and Dyfrig, to persuade David to come. It is said that when David addressed the synod, a snow-white dove descended from Heaven to sit on his shoulder, while the ground on which he stood was miraculously raised into a hill so that he could be better seen and heard.

David's eloquence was such that he was pressed to become primate of the Welsh Church, an office he only accepted on condition that the primatial seat be moved to Mynyw. This may have been an act of prudence, for the traditional seat at Caerleon on the River Usk was much farther east and exposed to the risk of pagan incursions from England.

There are many legends about David. One is that an angel appeared to his father, foretelling the saint's birth and instructing Sant to prepare gifts of a stag, a fish and a honeycomb. The honeycomb symbolised his honeyed wisdom, the fish his simple life of bread and water, and the stag his power to stamp on "serpents" such as the Pelagian heresy. It is even said that Saint Patrick thought of settling near Mynyw, until a voice told him the valley was reserved for a child yet unborn.

When David died at Mynyw *c.* 589, it is said that Saint Kentigern was at Llanelwy and saw his soul being borne to Heaven by angels.

COMGALL OF BANGOR

Comgall was born *c.* 516 in the Irish kingdom of Dalriada, and studied under Saint Fintan of Clonenagh, Co. Laois. While there, he is said to have restored a blind man's sight by pressing saliva to his eyes. In later life, he is said to have spat into a beggar's pocket, where a gold ring immediately appeared.

Comgall returned to the northern province of Ulster, living first on an island in Lough Erne, Co. Fermanagh, where the regime was so austere that seven companions died of cold and hunger. He then moved to Bangor, Co. Down, founding a monastery which attracted thousands of monks. Among them were Saints Columbanus, Gall and Moluag.

Curiously, despite the fact that Comgall allowed himself only one meal a day, many of his miracles concerned food. In one instance thieves became blind after stealing the monastery's vegetables, and when an ungenerous farmer refused to let the monks have grain, it was devoured by mice.

The saint died *c.* 501, following illnesses which some said were a punishment for the severity of Bangor's discipline.

COLUMBA OF IONA

There are several accounts of Columba's life, all attesting to the miraculous signs which preceded his birth at Gartan, Co. Donegal, in 521. An angel assured his mother that she would bear a son of great beauty who would be remembered among the Lord's prophets. Saint Buite, the dying abbot of Monasterboice in Co. Louth, is said to have foretold the birth of "a child illustrious before God and men". Columba was of royal blood. His father Phelim was of the Uí Néill clan and descended from the famous Niall of the Nine Hostages, while his mother Eithne was descended from a king of Leinster.

It was the custom for the children of ruling families to be fostered, but unusually Columba was put into the care of a priest. The boy's daily practice of reading the psalms led his young contemporaries to call him Columcille (Colum of the church) and he is more usually known by that name in Ireland. He went on to study under Saint Finnian of Moville, Co. Down, where his prayers are said to have turned spring water into communion wine. He later became a pupil of Saint Finnian of Clonard and was destined to become the most famous of the latter's "twelve apostles of Ireland". Columba also spent time with a Leinster bard named

Gemman, in whose company he witnessed the murder of a young girl and vowed that as the girl's soul went to Heaven the murderer's soul would go to Hell. When the murderer immediately died, Columba's reputation spread rapidly.

Columba established his first monastery at Derry in 548. Others followed, notably Durrow in Co. Offaly, which became famous for the Celtic artistry of its illuminated manuscripts. In 563 Columba sailed with twelve followers to found a monastery on the Scottish island of Iona, which was part of the Scottish kingdom of Dalriada, ruled by his cousin Conaill.

Legend has it that Columba's exile was an act of penance, and that he deliberately chose an island out of sight of his beloved Ireland. During a visit to Moville, Columba is said to have secretly copied a book of psalms. When Finnian discovered this, he insisted on having the copy. Columba refused to hand it over, and their dispute was referred to the high king, Diarmuid, who ruled: "To every cow her calf, and to every book its copy". Columba already resented Diarmuid for slaying a youth to whom the saint had given sanctuary and he persuaded his kinsmen to wage war. Diarmuid was defeated at Cuildreimhne, Co. Sligo and Columba was blamed for the hundreds of dead. When a synod called on him to make amends by converting an equal number of pagans, he opted to work among the Picts of Scotland.

The extent of Columba's missionary work has probably been exaggerated by his early biographers, but there is no doubting the profound influence of Iona on the Celtic Church as a whole, and on the spread of Christianity in Scotland and northern England. Columba was also a political figure of consequence. His early conversion of Brude, king of the Picts, reduced the threat of attacks on Christian Dalriada. In 575, returning to Ulster for a convention held at Drum Ceatt, he negotiated the Scottish kingdom's independence from the Irish Dalriada. At the same convention he persuaded King Aedh to preserve the bards of Ireland, whose satires had made them unpopular.

Columba died on Iona in 597. Chronicles of his life appeared in the following century, most notably from Saint Adomnán, who attributed to him many prophecies, visions and miracles, not least of which was warding off the Loch Ness monster with the sign of the cross.

KENTIGERN OF GLASGOW

According to legend, Kentigern was the illegitimate son of a Scottish princess. When her pregnancy was discovered she was cast out to sea in a frail coracle. She reached shore at Culross, on the Firth of Forth, where her son was born. He was baptised and educated at Culross by Saint Servanus, who gave him the name Mungo (dearest friend) by which he is commonly known. When jealous pupils tried to blame the boy for the death of a robin they had killed, Kentigern replaced its severed head and made the sign of the cross, whereupon the bird flew away.

Kentigern founded a monastery at Glasgow, where he was consecrated bishop. He preached throughout Cumbria, and is said to have founded a monastery at Llanelwy in Wales. When Saint Columba visited him at Glasgow, they exchanged pastoral staves as tokens of friendship. Kentigern died *c.* 612.

Kentigern's compassion is recalled in the legend of the queen who gave her lover a ring which she had received from her husband. The king took the ring from the sleeping lover and threw it in the River Clyde. He then demanded that his wife produce the gift. The distraught queen approached Kentigern, whose prayers were answered when the ring was found in a salmon's belly.

COLUMBANUS OF LUXEUIL

Of the many Celtic missionaries who chose "exile for Christ" on the European mainland, Columbanus was by far the most influential. Born in Leinster *c.* 543, he left home to study under a monk named Sinell on Cleenish Island in Lough Erne. He then spent many years at Bangor before receiving Saint Comgall's permission to sail to Europe *c.* 589 with twelve companions. They landed near Saint Malo, in Brittany.

The monks quickly established a reputation for their preaching and piety in a region which, though nominally Christian, had suffered sorely from wars and from the neglect of bishops. Columbanus was soon summoned to the court of Guthram, the Frankish king of Burgundy, who encouraged him to establish a monastery in the Vosges mountains.

After some exploration Columbanus chose to build on the ruins of a Roman fort at Annegray. He is said to have had his own retreat in a bear's den. Imposing a severe discipline, as at Bangor, Columbanus attracted so many followers that he soon built new monasteries at nearby Luxeuil, which became the principal foundation, and Fontaine. He drew up a series of rules, *Regula Monachorum*, requiring strict obedience to the abbot and a life of poverty and mortification through constant fasting. Great emphasis was laid on confession of sins followed by penances, with breaches of discipline punished by beatings with a leather strap. During the following century more than 100 monasteries were established under these rules, but eventually they gave way to the less exacting Rule of Saint Benedict.

Inevitably, Columbanus suffered from the hostility of Frankish bishops, who disapproved of some Irish practices. The Roman and Celtic Churches were notably divided on the method of calculating the date of Easter, and in adhering to the Celtic practice Columbanus laid himself open to the charge of unorthodoxy. In 600 he defended himself in a letter to Pope Gregory, and in 603 refused to attend a synod at Chalon-sur-Saone, writing instead to the assembled bishops that he wished to "remain in silence in these woods and to live beside the bones of our seventeen dead brethren."

By now Theuderich II was on the throne of Burgundy, and Columbanus incurred his displeasure by refusing to bless the king's four illegitimate sons and pressing him to marry. Theuderich's grandmother, Queen Brunhilde, feared losing her influence to a new queen and became an implacable foe. In 610 Theuderich ordered the expulsion of Columbanus and all other Irish monks. They were taken under armed guard to the port of Nantes, some 600 miles away to be shipped back to Ireland. However, their ship immediately ran aground, and the captain took this as a sign that the monks should be disembarked.

After further travels, Columbanus reached Metz, where King

Theudebert II offered his protection and encouraged the saint to work among the pagan tribes around the Swiss lakes. He settled briefly at Bregenz, near Lake Constance, but was forced to move on when Theudebert was defeated in battle by his brother Theuderich. This precipitated a quarrel with Saint Gall, the only survivor of the twelve monks who left Bangor, who disobeyed Columbanus by remaining in Switzerland.

Crossing the Alps into Lombardy *c.* 613, Columbanus was welcomed at Milan by King Agilulf, who offered him land at Bobbio in the foothills of the Apennines. Despite his age Columbanus took an active part in building the new monastery, which became famous for its library. His last act, on his death-bed in 615, was to send his abbot's staff to Gall as a token of forgiveness.

DYMPNA OF GHEEL

So much of Dympna's story has the ring of a folk-tale that it is impossible to separate fact and fiction. This seventh century saint was supposedly the daughter of a pagan Celtic chieftain, probably Irish, and a Christian mother. After his wife's death the grieving chieftain conceived a passion for his daughter because she resembled her mother, and he sought to marry her. Horrified, Dympna fled with her chaplain, Saint Gerebernus. They settled at Gheel, near the Belgian city of Antwerp, where Dympna devoted herself to helping the poor and the sick. They were discovered by her father, who had traced them through coins spent on their journey. When Dympna continued to reject the unnatural marriage, her father slew Gerebernus and severed her head.

According to legend, many miracles occurred where the martyrs' blood was shed. Local people also discovered two marble tombs which they believed angels had brought in honour of the saints. Many cures for madness and epilepsy were attributed to Dympna's intercession and in the thirteenth century the bishop of Cambrai commissioned a *Life of Dympna* which drew on oral tradition. Today she is Belgium's patron saint of the insane, and for centuries Gheel has been noted for the care and treatment of the mentally ill.

Fursey of Péronne

Son of an Irish prince, Fursey became abbot of a monastery in Tuam, Co. Galway, but it was as a missionary in England and France that he achieved a European fame overshadowed only by Columbanus. He was welcomed to East Anglia *c.* 630 by King Sigebert, who granted land for a monastery at Burgh Castle in Suffolk. Becoming ill, Fursey fell into a trance and, according to Saint Bede the historian, quit his body from evening till cock-crow and was found worthy to behold the chorus of angels in Heaven. Fursey's visions of Heaven and Hell, experienced throughout his life and widely recounted, are thought to have inspired Dante's *Divine Comedy*.

After some years in East Anglia, Fursey set out on a pilgrimage to Rome. He was well-received by Clovis, king of the Franks, whose palace mayor, Erconwald, persuaded the saint to build a monastery at Lagny, outside Paris. Fursey died *c.* 648 at Mazerolles, where he had once miraculously restored a nobleman's son to life. Erconwald had the body brought to Péronne in Picardy, where it awaited entombment while a new church was built. Four years later, when the body was buried near the altar, it was found to be completely free from decomposition.

AIDAN OF LINDISFARNE

During the seventh century Northumbria, comprising the kingdoms of Bernicia and Deira, was a battleground in which the fate of rival kings determined whether the Celtic or the Roman Church should be the prevailing missionary influence. In 616, when King Ethelfrith of Northumbria was defeated in battle and slain, his son Oswald took refuge in Scotland and was converted to Christianity at Iona. Edwin, the new king, also became a Christian, but under the influence of Saint Paulinus, bishop of York, whose allegiance was to Rome. After Edwin's death in 633, Paulinus abandoned his work in northern England. Oswald returned from exile and eventually became king, whereupon he sent to Iona for a bishop who would preach the Gospel in Northumbria.

The first Celtic bishop, Corman, soon returned to Iona, where he declared that the Angles of Northumbria were too stubborn and intractable. The historian Bede writes that, at a meeting to discuss the problem, an Irish monk called Aidan suggested that Corman had been unreasonably harsh with his unlearned listeners, and "did not first, as the Apostle has taught us, offer them the milk of less solid doctrine." It was immediately resolved to send Aidan to

Northumbria as bishop.

Little is known of the saint's early life, save that he may have studied under Saint Senan on Scattery Island, Co. Clare. He arrived in Northumbria c. 635 and with Oswald's consent made his headquarters on the offshore island of Lindisfarne, close to Oswald's castle at Bamburgh. It was a fruitful partnership, with Oswald having on occasion to interpret the words of Aidan, who lacked fluency in the English language.

When Oswald was killed in battle in 642, Aidan worked equally well with Oswin, king of Deira. Aidan preached widely throughout Northumbria, travelling on foot, so that he could readily talk to everyone he met. When Oswin gave him a horse for use in difficult terrain, Aidan quixotically gave it to a beggar soliciting alms. Oswin was angry until, as Bede recounts, Aidan asked if the son of a mare was more precious to the king than a son of God. Oswin sought Aidan's pardon, and promised never again to question or regret any of his wealth being given away to children of God. Both Oswald and Oswin are venerated in England as saints and martyrs.

Scores of Scottish and Irish monks assisted Aidan in his missionary work, building churches and spreading Celtic Christian influence to a degree that Lindisfarne became the virtual capital of Christian England. The saint also recruited classes of Anglo-Saxon youths to be educated at Lindisfarne. Among them was Saint Eata, abbot of Melrose and later of Lindisfarne. In time, Eata's pupil, Saint Cuthbert, also became bishop of Lindisfarne.

Aidan lived a frugal life, and encouraged the laity to fast and

study the scriptures. He himself fasted on Wednesdays and Fridays, and seldom ate at the royal table. When a feast was set before him he would give the food away to the hungry. The presents he received were given to the poor or used to buy the freedom of slaves, some of whom entered the priesthood. During Lent Aidan would retire to the small island of Farne for prayer and penance. While there in 651, he saw smoke rising from Bamburgh, which was then under attack by the pagan King Penda of Mercia. He prayed for the wind to change, and many of the besiegers were destroyed by fire.

When Oswin was killed in 651 by his treacherous cousin Oswy, king of Bernica, Aidan was grief-stricken. The Saint outlived Oswin by a mere twelve days, dying in a shelter he had erected against the wall of his church in Bamburgh.

FIACRE OF MEAUX

Fiacre, one of the most venerated saints of medieval France, was born in Ireland, where he was probably christened Fiachra. He and a few followers arrived, *c.* 626, in the French diocese of Meaux, where he built a hermitage and where he remained until his death *c.* 670. It is said that the bishop, Saint Faro, promised Fiacre as much land as he could dig in a day. A local woman complained that he was digging too rapidly, and thereafter Fiacre excluded all women from his chapel on pain of blindness or madness.

He quickly acquired a reputation for sanctity and for miraculous healing powers. So often did he cure one ailment, an ulcerous condition, that it became known as Saint Fiacre's Disease. He was probably the first abbot to set up a hospice for Irish pilgrims, often as penniless as they were numerous, beside his monastery. A curved stone on which he had once sat attracted pilgrims seeking relief from haemorrhoids.

Fiacre was skilful in cultivating plants, many with medicinal properties, and he is patron saint of France's gardeners. He has also given his name to the horse-drawn, four-wheel *fiacre* cabs, which first appeared in seventeenth-century Paris outside the Hotel Saint-Fiacre.

GALL OF SAINT GALL

Like Columbanus, Gall was born in Leinster and experienced the severe monastic regime at Bangor. Joining Columbanus on his voyage to France, he served him faithfully until they parted acrimoniously at Bregenz in Switzerland in 612. When Gall insisted that a fever made him unfit for the difficult journey to Italy, the authoritarian Columbanus imposed on him a penance of never celebrating Mass during the older saint's lifetime. Gall observed this until 615, when he had a vision of Columbanus's death and offered Mass for the repose of his soul. He sent his astonished deacon Magnoald to Bobbio, whence he returned with the dead Columbanus's staff.

Nursed at Arbon by a sympathetic priest named Willemar, Gall regained his health and built a hermitage beside the River Steinach. There, it is said, he ordered a bear to go into the woods and collect firewood. The main credit for spreading Christianity among the Alemanni tribes belongs to Gall and his followers, and from small beginnings emerged the great medieval abbey of Saint Gall. He refused invitations to become bishop of Constance and abbot of Luxeuil, preferring to continue the mission he had begun after parting from Columbanus. Gall died at Arbon *c.* 640.

COLMAN OF LINDISFARNE

Colman became the third abbot-bishop of Lindisfarne in 661, succeeding Saints Aidan and Finan. Like them, he had come from Ireland to become a monk at Iona, and he wholly favoured Celtic custom in such matters as the dating of Easter and the tonsure of monks. He had the support of Oswy, king of Northumbria, but Oswy's queen, Enfleda, came from Essex and favoured the Roman Church's practices. In 664 Oswy summoned the Synod of Whitby to decide the issues. Colman was defeated in debate by Saint Wilfrid of Ripon and resigned.

He returned to Iona, accompanied by his Irish monks and by thirty English monks, but then decided to settle in Ireland. Divisions soon appeared at the new monastery on Inishbofin, an island off the coast of Co. Galway. The English monks complained that the Irish visited the mainland in summer, leaving them to bring in the harvest alone. Colman solved the problem by establishing a new foundation for the English monks on the mainland. He died on Inishbofin in 676. Roman practices had already gained sway in southern England, and Colman's defeat at Whitby presaged the gradual decline of the Celtic Church, though in Ireland Roman authority was not fully established until the twelfth century.

INDEX

The major references to saints' lives are in bold type. Common variants on saints' names (principally in English, Irish, Welsh or Latin) are given in brackets.